Ju

Decorating
for Tweens & Teens

Gloria Hander Lyons

Blue Sage Press

Just Fun Decorating
for Tweens & Teens

Inquires should be addressed to:
Blue Sage Press
48 Borondo Pines
La Marque, TX 77568
www.BlueSagePress.com

ISBN-13: 978-0-9790618-3-7
ISBN-10: 0-9790618-3-0

Library of Congress Control Number: 2007902088

First Edition: April, 2007

Printed in the United States of America

Table of Contents

Introduction
Just Fun Decorating for Tweens and Teens

Your room should be a comfortable retreat—a place where you can escape from the hectic world outside. It should reflect your personality and favorite activities in addition to providing the necessary furniture, storage and lighting to meet your functional needs.

But decorating involves more than just comfort and function. It's also about adding beauty and joy to your life.

If you aren't happy with the current state of your décor, or feel that you room isn't "working" for you, keep reading. You might just find the answers to your decorating dilemmas in the next few chapters.

This book offers helpful hints, money saving tips and fun ideas for furniture layouts, color schemes, lighting, window treatments, theme rooms, designer tricks, accessorizing and more.

You'll learn creative tips for customizing your décor using fun do-it-yourself projects to help make your room more functional, as well as more beautiful—a place where you'll enjoy spending time.

Don't be afraid to express yourself when it comes to decorating. Create a space that makes you happy, based on your own personal style—not popular trends or someone else's opinions. Decorate your room using the items you love; things that will make you feel good every time see them.

The suggestions, tips and fun ideas presented in this book can help you design a more attractive, comfortable and inviting space.

Whether you plan to rearrange the furniture and accessories you already have or want to start over with an entirely new design, you can give your room a whole new look and feel.

A Room Without a Cause

Many times a room isn't "working" for us because we simply haven't thought about how we need it to function; therefore, the room doesn't have the right furniture or lighting to meet our needs.

Do you want a comfortable chair with good lighting in your room for reading? Do you need more places for friends to sit? Where could you squeeze in a desk for homework?

Don't live with the frustration of doing without—fix the problem. Before starting any new decorating project, take the time to decide how you need your space to function.

This task isn't hard. Just take a few moments to decide what activities you'll be doing in your room. Of course you'll need a bed for sleeping, but would you also like to include an additional sleeping area for when you have a friend stay over? Do you need more storage for books or clothes?

Taking the time to think about how you need your room to function will help you decide what furniture pieces and lighting you'll need. Make a list of these items. Then, simply remove any pieces of furniture that don't meet your needs and replace them with ones that work.

Are you planning to do an interior re-design, where you'll be using the furniture and accessories you already own, or do you plan to purchase all new pieces or just a few new items?

If you're doing an interior re-design, you'll need to "shop" your entire house to find furniture and lighting to make your room more functional. Use the tips on pages 52-56 for refinishing lamps and painting furniture.

If you want to add new furniture, use the list you made earlier, so you'll know what pieces to buy.

Don't just "make do" with the way your room is set up now. Take the time to figure out how you need it to function and make it "work" for you!

Helpful Hints:

- If you want to add a new piece of furniture to your room, be sure to measure the space where you plan to place it to make sure it will fit. AND don't forget to measure the doors into your room to make sure you can get the piece inside. If you plan to purchase a tall piece of furniture, measure the ceiling height in your room, as well.

- If you want an extra bed in your room for friends to sleep over, add a pull-out trundle bed that is stored underneath your bed and rolls out when you need it. If you have space for an upholstered chair in your room, get one that folds out into a bed. A less expensive option is a self-inflatable air mattress that you can store underneath your bed until company arrives.

- If you need extra seating when you have friends over but don't have space in your room for regular chairs, purchase folding directors chairs that can be stored in the closet or underneath your bed until company arrives. They have fabric seats and backs which are fun to decorate using acrylic paints and stencils or rubber stamps to match your room's décor.

Money-Saving Tip:

- If you're crafty, scout garage sales, flea markets and second-hand stores for furniture, lighting and accessories that might meet your needs, then refinish, paint or recover the items to match your décor.

Fun Idea:

- Plan a decorating party. Invite a couple of your friends over to help re-design your room. Whether they are helping you rearrange your furniture or painting the walls, it will make the work more fun.

  Offer to help redecorate their rooms, as well, using the information you learn from this book. It could start you off in the direction of a whole new career.

What's the Point?

When planning the design for your room, think about what feature you could showcase as your focal point. Do you have an attractive arched window in your room that you might want to frame with curtain panels? Do you want your bed to be the center of attention? Do you want to display a collection of your favorite artwork over a seating area or desk?

Taking the time to create a special focal point in your room will make the time you spend there more enjoyable. That is, after all, what decorating is about—adding more beauty to our lives.

The focal point of any room should instantly draw your attention. When using a piece of furniture, like a sofa or desk as the base for your focal point, arrange a group of accessories, such as framed mirrors or prints, vases, lamps and other objects on, beside or above the piece to create a pleasing composition and make your focal point more attractive. Look at the example in Figure 1.

7

Figure 1

When creating a focal point using wall art above a piece of furniture, try to make the composition large enough in scale and extended high enough on the wall to establish its importance.

How do you know if your arrangement works? Just stand back and take a good look. Does the composition appear pleasing and fairly well balanced? Does it create enough of an impact to draw your attention? As long as you're happy with the results and you've taken the time to check the overall impact, then go with it!

Painting an accent wall in a darker or more vibrant color is another way to make your arrangement stand out. Placing any object in front of a sharply contrasting color makes it more visible. In the example above, if the room was painted a light beige color, and the sofa and artwork on the wall above it were also light in color, then painting the wall behind them in a darker shade of beige, or one of the accent colors in the room, such as medium blue, would make the furniture and artwork stand out. Your focal point would have more of an impact.

If you have a window with a beautiful view, make it the focal point of your room. Frame the window with drapery panels or fabric swags that will draw your eye towards it.

Add even more interest to your composition with a small seating area arranged in front of the window if you have enough space, or place a small bench underneath. Look at the example shown in the drawing below.

When using your bed as the focal point, you can hang curtain panels gathered onto a curtain rod behind the headboard of your bed to create more of an impact.

You can also hang a wreath on the wall above your headboard and drape a length of fabric through it that hangs down on each side of your bed.

A canopy bed with fabric panels draped over the top and down the sides can also create a beautiful focal point.

Painting a wall mural depicting a favorite scene or a design from your bedding is another way to create a focal point.

This is a fun and easy way to add your own unique style to your room. See the instructions on page 12 for painting decorative designs on walls, furniture, cabinets and more.

Choose a focal point for your room, whether it's your bed, a window with an attractive view, an arrangement of artwork over a piece of furniture, or a wall mural and create a beautiful composition to enjoy.

Decorative Painting Instructions

Personalizing your room with hand painted murals and other designs is not only fun, but easy and inexpensive to do. Want a window with a view? Paint one. Want a room full of flowers? Paint them.

Painting scenes on your walls, floors, furniture and doors is as easy as coloring in a coloring book. Just find the design you want, trace it onto tracing paper, enlarge it on a copy machine or computer and transfer it to the surface you want to paint.

You can also use an opaque projector for very large designs to project the image onto the wall surface and trace it. Then fill in the traced design with acrylic paints.

There are hundreds of painting books and magazines that feature design patterns. These books will tell you what color paints to purchase and give you painting directions to complete your design.

You can also find easy to paint designs in coloring books and children's books. For a customized decorating look, copy designs from your curtains, bedding or wallpaper and paint them on your walls or furniture.

There are an unlimited number of possibilities for hand painted designs. All that's required is imagination and a little work to make your room as unique as your own personality.

Preparing the Surface:

The first step in any painting project is to prepare the surface properly. If you're painting a scene on a textured drywall surface (typical in most homes), be sure the wall is freshly painted with wall paint that has a "flat finish". The acrylic paints that you will be using to paint your design won't stick to a shiny surface such as high-gloss or semi-gloss paint. A light background color on the walls is best.

If you're painting on a wooden surface with a shiny finish, such as furniture, cabinets or doors, first wash the surface to remove any dirt or grease. Use a damp (not soaking) cloth moistened with a solution of water and detergent. Let dry. Next sand the surface lightly with a fine grit sandpaper and remove any dust with a damp paper towel. Then, using a paint brush, or sponge roller for a smoother finish, apply a coat of primer (found at the home improvement store) and let dry thoroughly.

Lightly sand the surface again, remove any dust, and apply the desired color of paint for your base coat, which is the background color for your painted design. Let the base coat dry thoroughly before tracing your design onto the surface.

Preparing the Design Pattern:

Before you can make the pattern for your creative masterpiece, you must decide what you want to paint. Do you want to create a fantasy garden by painting flowers all around the room? Do you want to paint a beautiful landscape on the wall? Do you want to add a design from your bedding to your walls or the top of a table or chest of drawers?

Whatever design you choose, you'll need to find a clear picture of it. Use tracing paper and a pencil to trace the design and then go over the lines again with a black permanent marker to make them darker.

Next, decide how large you want to make the design. Do you want one large scene on a wall, or a small design on each corner of a tabletop? Take the traced design to a copy store and enlarge it to the size you need or use your computer to scan and enlarge your design.

After enlarging your design to the desired size, position the pattern on the wall or furniture piece and secure it with painter's tape. Slip a piece of graphite paper (found in craft stores) underneath the pattern and trace over the lines of the design using a stylus or empty ballpoint pen.

Remove the pattern and graphite paper and you're ready to paint. If you plan to use the same pattern many times, such as tracing a roomful of butterflies, make more than one copy of your pattern.

If you want your design to cover an entire wall, use an opaque projector to project the image onto the wall and trace the design with a pencil. Just remember, you don't want the design or mural to be so large that it overwhelms the room. You can purchase opaque projectors at most craft stores fairly inexpensively.

Painting Supplies:

Decide on the colors of acrylic paints that you'll need. You can purchase these paints in 2-ounce bottles at craft stores.

You'll also need to get several sizes of artist's paintbrushes, depending on the size of your design. Moderately priced brushes intended for use with acrylic paints are fine. Get flat brushes for filling in large areas of paint and round brushes for smaller areas.

You'll also need disposable plastic cups for holding your paint while painting or for mixing paint if you want a custom color. Keep plenty of paper towels on hand for drying off wet brushes and wiping up spills or drips.

Be sure to cover the floor with a painter's plastic drop cloth before you begin painting. It's also helpful to have some touch-up wall-color paint available to touch up any drips on the wall after you've finished painting your mural.

After filling in all the colored areas of your design with paint, you might also want to outline your artwork to make the design more "crisp". To do this, use a permanent marker or paint pen in black or a dark color that coordinates with your design.

Protecting the Finished Design:

If your paint project is on a wall, you don't need to seal the design. However, if it is on cabinet doors or furniture, seal it with several coats of clear acrylic sealer, either from a spray can (follow the directions on the can) or the kind that is applied with a brush or roller.

If your design is painted on the floor, then seal it with several coats of polyurethane to protect it from wear.

It's Just Paint!

Don't be afraid to get creative and add your own personal artistic touch to your room and furniture. After all, it's just paint! If you don't like the result, you can always paint over it.

Solving the Puzzle

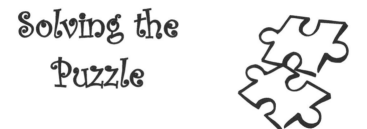

After deciding what pieces of furniture you'll need in your room, the next step is arranging it in your space. Most teens' rooms include: a bed (usually twin size), a night stand, a small desk and desk chair, a bookcase and a dresser or chest of drawers with a mirror above it.

Your list of furniture needs will vary, depending on the size of your room and additional furniture you might want to add for other activities, like an armoire or stand for a television or additional seating for friends.

Since the bed is the largest piece of furniture in the room and will probably be your focal point, decide where you want to place it before adding any other furniture pieces. It is usually placed on one of the longest walls in the room, but if you have the space, you can also angle it in a corner. This positioning creates a sense of motion rather than the more static feel of furniture placed square with the walls. Either choice is fine as long as you are pleased with the arrangement.

If you plan to use the bed for your focal point, you'll want to place it in a spot that is visible when you enter the room—not tucked away in a blind corner.

Two furniture layout possibilities are shown on page 18.

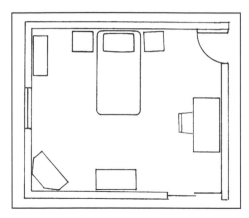

In this layout, the bed is anchored against the longest wall with a nightstand on each side. There is an armoire in the corner for the television, a bookcase on the left wall, a desk and a chest of drawers across from the bed.

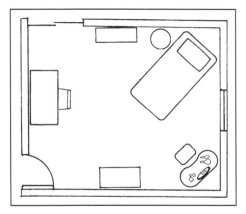

In this layout, the bed is angled in the corner with a side table beside it. There is a vanity in the corner, a chest of drawers on the bottom wall, a bookcase on the top wall and a desk.

Arrange the furniture pieces you need in your space. Try to distribute the furniture evenly around the room as shown in the examples above. When you're finished, stand back and observe the visual weight and size of the furniture placed throughout the room.

Do you have too many large (or visually heavy) pieces on one side of the room, making it feel out of balance? Do you have any empty corners that need to be decorated? If so, make a few adjustments and add objects as needed to try to make the furniture layout feel more balanced.

After placing all your furniture pieces in the room, check the layout for overall balance and add objects such as plants, screens, benches, small tables, etc. to any areas that might seem bare.

Traffic Patterns:

While creating your new furniture arrangement, take note of where the traffic patterns are in the room, so you'll remember to leave these areas free of furniture.

- Try to avoid placing any large pieces of furniture close to the entrance to the room which might create a road block for traffic.

- Make sure there is enough room to walk through the space comfortably without bumping into furniture. Traffic paths should be about three feet wide if possible.

- Make sure you can open door to the room's entrance and closet doors fully without bumping into furniture. Also check to see that you can open drawers easily without bumping into other furniture.

Examples of furniture arrangements that might cause traffic flow problems are listed below:

1. Overcrowding your room with too much furniture. Solution: Refer to the furniture list you created when deciding on the function of the room. Remove any pieces of furniture that aren't absolutely necessary.

2. Using furniture that is too large for the space. Solution: Trade them out with smaller pieces in your home, purchase new ones that are more suitable in scale, or reduce the number of pieces in the room.

3. Too many small, inefficient storage units. Solution: Try to consolidate the items you need to store into larger units that take up less floor space. For example: Use one tall bookcase instead of two short ones.

Try arranging the furniture in your room to create a more comfortable and functional space. After creating your layout, check to see that the furniture is distributed evenly throughout the room.

Pay careful attention to where the traffic patterns are, and place your furniture to promote a comfortable flow. An inviting furniture layout should draw you into the space—not put up a road-block in your path. Arrange your furniture so that it welcomes you into the room.

Helpful Hint:

Try to balance the number of wood and upholstered pieces you use in the room. Too many hard surfaces make the space feel cold and uninviting. Use fabrics, plants (real or silk), rugs, pillows, throws, etc. to add softness and warmth.

Slightly Off-Kilter

Balance is a very important element when decorating a room. Whether referring to the placement of furniture, color or lighting, it's important to distribute them evenly throughout the space, or the room will feel off balance.

In addition to distributing the furniture evenly around the room, you should also check for balance in the height of the furniture pieces in the room. This doesn't mean that all the furniture should be the same height. What you want is a mixture of heights—some tall objects and some low objects, to create an interesting mix.

After deciding on your furniture layout, simply check to see that the taller pieces are dispersed evenly around the room, otherwise, the room will feel out of balance.

If you have a tall piece of furniture on one wall, try to balance it on the opposite wall with another tall piece of furniture, or a lower piece of furniture with artwork or shelves arranged over it that will create enough visual weight on the wall to balance the taller piece of furniture.

For example, if you hang curtains on the wall behind your bed to create a focal point, you might balance the height and visual weight of the bed arrangement with a tall bookcase or a dresser with a mirror above it on the wall opposite the bed.

Balance is important in creating harmony in your space. We have already discussed distributing your furniture evenly around the room when arranging your furniture.

We also talked about creating a focal point by displaying decorative items on your focal point wall in an attractive composition that appears balanced. Use this same technique to achieve balance for all the "wall elevations" (how the furniture appears when placed in front of a wall).

An example of a balanced arrangement on a wall elevation is listed below:

1. Start by placing the largest piece of furniture in the center of the wall. In this example, we'll use a desk.

2. Place other furniture pieces or objects that have approximate visual balance on either side.

3. Create a balanced display of artwork on the wall over the piece of furniture or on either side of it as shown below.

Visual Weight:

On the previous pages, we talked about distributing your furniture evenly around your room to create balance, based on the visual weight of the furniture pieces. We also discussed arranging wall art and accessories in a balanced composition on a wall elevation.

Visual Weight in Accessories:

An example of comparing the visual weight of objects you might use as accessories is two table lamps that are exactly the same height, but the base of one lamp is thin, like a turned wooden base, and the other has a fuller shape, like a Ginger jar.

Look at the example below. The lamp with the fuller-shaped base appears to have more visual weight than the thinner lamp base.

Visual Weight in Furniture Pieces:

The same principle applies to furniture pieces. Even though the two end tables shown below have the same dimensions, the glass table has less visual weight than the chest of drawers.

If you wanted to use the two tables above on either end of a sofa or each side of a bed, the arrangement would not feel balanced. Another element to consider when using unmatched furniture pieces in the same arrangement is the style of the furniture. The glass table is contemporary in style and the chest of drawers is more traditional.

Unless you were going for a transitional or eclectic mood in your room (see pages 75 and 76 for descriptions), you would want to choose furniture that is similar in style.

Keep these factors in mind when arranging the furniture and accessories in your room. You don't need to use matching furniture pieces in your arrangements, but try to keep the visual weight of your objects in balance and use similar furniture style pieces.

Striving for balance, both in your furniture layout, as well as in your wall elevations will make your room feel more harmonious and inviting.

Setting the Mood

Have you ever felt that being in a room had a negative effect on your mood, but you didn't know why? Three things that affect the mood of a room are: color, style of furnishings, and lighting. Color is a very powerful decorating tool, and since the walls are the largest surface in any room, painting them is the least expensive but most dramatic change you can make. Color can completely transform the mood of any room, which affects the way you feel when you're in it.

You can use color to make a room feel bright or dark, cheerful or solemn, dramatic or casual, exciting or serene. Color can also create optical illusions to make small rooms seem more spacious or large rooms seem cozier. With the right color of paint, it's easy to camouflage a room's defects and highlight its positive features.

Even on a limited budget, using just the right color can bring a room to life. What mood do you want to create in your room? Choosing your color scheme is simple once you make this decision.

When planning a color scheme, you first need to decide whether you want to use cool or warm colors in your room. Cool colors are blue, green and violet. Warm colors are red, orange and yellow.

The natural light in your room can help you decide whether your color scheme should be warm or cool. If your room doesn't get any direct sunlight because it faces north, then the natural light in the room will be cool. Therefore, you might want to use warm colors in the room. If your room faces south and gets lots of sunlight, you might want to use cool colors.

Choose your color scheme according to the mood you want to create. Do you want to wake up to a warm and cheery yellow on the walls? Or do you prefer a soothing, serene green or blue? You can also choose a neutral color like taupe as a background for bright, bold-colored accessories.

Once you've decided on the mood you want to use in the room, you're ready to select the specific colors for your scheme. A color scheme can be built around one color or two or three colors. When using more than one color, however, it's best to choose one of them as the main color (the one you will paint on the walls), and use the other one or two colors as accents (for upholstery, window treatments and accessories). And try to distribute your accent colors evenly around the room to for balance.

You can create a color scheme from colors you like or from colors in the upholstered furniture or bedding you already own. You might also choose colors from an "inspiration piece", such as artwork, an area rug or a piece of fabric.

An easy way to choose your color scheme from an inspiration piece is to choose the lightest color in the artwork or fabric to paint the walls. Use one of the medium colors for a few of your solid-color upholstered furniture pieces and/or draperies. Pick one of the brightest colors for accents in the form of accessories, such as vases, throw pillows, frames, etc.

If you want to create a mood that represents a specific decorating style or theme, such as Seaside or Shabby Chic, then choose colors that are authentic to that particular style. A few palettes are listed below, but it's easy to gather this type of information from the internet or books at your local library for whatever style you like.

English Cottage style suggests pinks and greens in delicate floral prints, stripes and plaids. Elegant chintz fabric contrasts with the texture of wood, iron and stone. Furniture is casual and rustic, softened with comfy fabric cushions and easy-care slip covers. Accessories include delicate china, landscape paintings, colorful rugs, crystal candleholders and vases filled with flowers.

Seaside color schemes use aqua blue, sandy tan and sea glass green with touches of pale, driftwood gray. Furniture is casual and comfy wicker, rattan or painted wood with sturdy fabrics or washable slipcovers. Window treatments are airy and light. Accessories include seashells of every size, shape and color, as well as nautical themed items, such as prints or figurines of wooden boats, lighthouses, portholes, fishing nets and beach scenes.

Shabby Chic décor uses delicate colors, such as soft white, muted gray, pale pink and faded green. Furniture is usually painted white with sanded edges to make them appear worn. The look also includes soft floral fabrics, vintage lacy linens, mismatched china and crystal chandeliers.

Southwestern colors are cactus green, adobe red and sand-colored neutrals with accents of bright yellow, dusty orange and turquoise. Hand-painted tiles are used on walls and floors. Accessories include wrought iron and pottery. Furniture is over-sized and made of rustic wood and iron, upholstered in sturdy woven fabrics, leather and suede.

Romantic style features lots of silky, flowing fabrics, perhaps draped over the bed to form a canopy and over the windows to soften their hard, rectangular angles. Accessories include piles of accent pillows and throws on the bed and chairs. Colors are usually feminine pinks or pastels. Furniture is small scale and delicate.

Tropical color schemes include sky blue, olive green and warm brown with accents of red. Tropical décor features comfortable upholstered furniture and accessories made from animal and jungle prints, rattan, leather, wicker and grasscloth. Use bamboo or matchstick blinds or plantation shutters for window treatments. A large palm or banana plant, jungle-theme lamps and large-scale accessories complete your theme.

Western style décor features honey colored wood, gray stone and black wrought iron metal. Accent colors are can be brick red, terra cotta, forest green or navy. Western style furniture is often large scale and made of rustic wood. Fabrics and accessories include rock, wood, metal, leather, wool, birch bark, beadwork, old Indian blankets and antlers.

When choosing colors for your walls, remember that dark colors make things seem smaller and closer. Therefore, dark colors can make a room seem smaller. Light colors make things seem larger and farther away, so light wall colors can make a room appear bigger.

To make a narrow room feel wider, paint the end walls a darker color, to make them appear to advance toward you, and use light colors on the long walls, to make them appear to recede into the distance.

After you have chosen the paint color for your walls, it's best to test it before painting the entire room. First, paint a piece of poster board and hang it on the wall. Observe how the color of the paint is affected by the natural light coming into the room at various times of the day. Also note how the color is affected by the artificial lighting in the room.

The color of the window treatments in the room can affect the appearance of the wall color, as well. Light filtering into the room through colored sheer curtains will change the color of the light.

If you're satisfied with your paint test, then go ahead and paint your room. If not, you'll need to make another choice.

If you aren't comfortable with a bold color change on your walls, add color to your room gradually. Use accent pillows, throws, area rugs and accessories to add color. Next, try painting one wall as an accent or adding more color with window treatments.

Don't ignore the power of color when decorating your room. Painting the walls is an inexpensive way to make a dramatic change. But choose your room's color scheme carefully, so it will have a positive effect on your mood and make the time you spend there more enjoyable.

Helpful Hints:

- If you want your color mood to be very warm or very cool, use an adjacent color scheme: two or three colors that are next to each other on the color wheel. For example: red and orange or blue, blue-green and green. If you want the mood to be more neutral, use a complementary color scheme, two colors that are directly opposite each other on the color wheel, such as red and green, blue and orange or yellow and violet.

- When deciding whether to use a light or dark wall color in your room, keep in mind that objects are more visible when placed against a sharply contrasting color background. Dark furniture placed against a light-colored wall will stand out more. If you want to camouflage an object (such as a piece of furniture that is too large for the space), place it in front of a similar colored background.

Fun Idea:

- To make a group of framed prints or three-dimensional objects you want to display on your wall stand out, paint a block of color on the wall where they will be displayed. First measure the area where you will hang the wall art, then mark it off using painter's tape. It can be a rectangle or square just large enough to fit your grouping. Paint inside the marked-off area using one of the accent colors for your room that will contrast with the wall art you want to display. Remove the tape before the paint is dry for cleaner edges. After the paint dries, hang your artwork and admire the results!

Floating Art & Other Mysteries

Accessories add warmth and interest to your room. This is also an area where you can express your own unique style, using objects that you've collected because they have special appeal. But it's important to use accessories that fit with the style, theme and color of the décor you've chosen in order to create a more harmonious feel.

When choosing the accessories for your room, pay careful attention to the mood each object projects. Does it match your décor? Do those silver, contemporary picture frames stick out like a sore thumb on your rustic country display shelf? With practice, you can train your eye to look for these details.

Hanging Wall Art:

Wall art accessories include paintings, framed prints, framed mirrors, wall screens and even some three dimensional objects such as sculptures, shelves and sconces. Wall art is an important part of the room's décor; therefore, it's important to display these pieces effectively.

A common tendency when displaying a piece of framed art is hanging it too high, so it looks like it's "floating" by itself on the wall. Hang wall art pieces low enough so they appear to be part of a grouping of furniture beneath them.

When displaying a piece of art over a sofa or chair, hang it only about eight to ten inches above the sofa back. Figure 2 shows an example of "floating" art. Compare it to Figure 3.

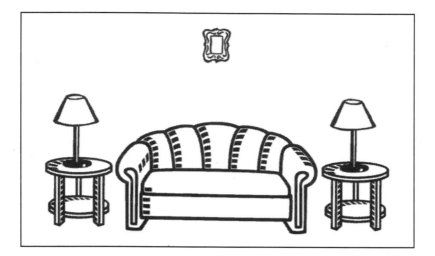

Figure 2

Figure 3

Wall art can help establish the focal point of a room. A focal point should create sufficient impact to draw your attention, such as a large framed mirror hung over a chest of drawers or a poster hung over your headboard.

When hanging a large piece of wall art, check to see that its scale and shape are a good fit for the space where it will be hung. For example, the shape of the wall space above a sofa or desk is usually a horizontal, rectangular shape. Therefore, the best shape for artwork to fit this space is a rectangular or oval shape, hung horizontally. If the wall space is square, use a square or round piece of artwork. The art in Figure 2 is not an appropriate shape for this space.

Next, check the size of the wall art. Does it appear to be too large for the scale of the furniture piece, or is it too small to create the impact you want? The art piece in Figure 2 is too small in scale for the size of the sofa. If you don't have one piece of artwork that is large enough, use several smaller pieces in a grouping.

When arranging a group of framed prints or photographs, hang them close enough together so they appear to be one unit, but not so close that the space looks crowded.

There is no magic formula for determining how far apart to place the artwork because it varies according to the size of the pieces. Just stand back and take a good look. Does the spacing feel right or does it need to be adjusted? Does the scale of the overall grouping fit the space you need to fill?

It's usually a good idea to choose a similar frame material for all the pictures in the grouping—gold, silver, wood, lacquer, etc. And pay attention to the frame styles, whether they are rustic, contemporary, traditional, etc. Do they fit with the style of the other furnishings in your room?

You can also mix framed prints or paintings with other interesting shapes such as framed mirrors, shelves, sculptures, etc. in one grouping. When arranging groups of decorative objects on a wall, it's helpful to create your arrangement on paper first.

Another way to create your layout is to trace the shapes of your frames or decorative objects onto paper, label them so you know which picture or object each one represents and cut them out. Use painter's tape to hang them on the wall and move them around until you get a look you like, then hang the wall art in place of each cutout.

Remember to balance the visual weight of the objects when creating your wall art arrangement. Avoid putting all the large objects on one side and the small ones on the other. It's also a good idea to place the larger objects on the bottom so the arrangement doesn't appear top-heavy.

Arranging Accessories in the Room:

The second category for accessories includes items such as vases, throw pillows, sculptures, plants, lamps and framed photographs, which are placed on the floor, tables, shelves, chairs or bed.

Remember to keep your decorating style or theme in mind when choosing the type of accessories you want to include in your room. Are the objects you've chosen suitable for the decorating style, color and mood or theme you want for your room?

When displaying small items, group similar objects together to create more of an impact.

These might be objects made up of similar materials, such as silver, crystal or wood, or theme-related items, like birdhouses, angels or trophies.

Group similar objects together for more impact

Scattering small items around the room creates a cluttered feel, so group these items together into collections. And remember, the smaller the items, the closer they need to be placed to the viewer. If you arrange a collection of small figurines on the top shelf of a tall bookcase, you won't be able to see them from such a distance.

Try not to put too many items in one display. This also creates a cluttered feel, and the objects aren't being shown off to their best advantage when they are crowded together.

If you have more accessories than you have display space, consider packing some of the objects away, then change them out occasionally with the ones currently out. You can change the look or theme of your room each time you rotate your accessories.

When arranging a group of accessories on a table or shelf, (also called a "tablescape"), use objects of varying heights, shapes, textures and sizes to create a more interesting composition, as shown at right.

Use attractive books or other objects to elevate some of the pieces to vary their heights. Just remember to place the tallest object in back and arrange the rest in descending order of size, so all the objects can be seen, as in the tablescape example above.

When displaying groups of framed photographs, it's best to use one type of material for all the frames in the group (wood, silver, copper, brass, lacquer, etc.) to create a cohesive look, but choose frames that complement the décor of the room.

When decorating a bookcase with a mixture of books and accessories, try not to overcrowd the shelves. Leave some space in your arrangement to avoid a cluttered look.

You can add beauty to your room by creating several attractive still life arrangements to enjoy.

- Stack an assortment of pretty fabric-covered hat boxes on top of an armoire.

- If you have a large collection of objects, such as trophies or dolls, install a narrow shelf around the entire perimeter of your room at door height to display your treasures in attractive groupings.

- Arrange a collection of baskets or plants under a side table.

- If you have a pleasing composition on one wall that you love to look at, place a mirror directly opposite the arrangement so you can enjoy the reflection as well.

Try to balance the soft and hard materials in your room. Too many hard surfaces make a room feel cold and uninviting. Use fabrics, plants (real or silk), rugs, pillows, and throws to add softness and warmth.

Area rugs are accessories for the floor. They add color, texture and design patterns to your space. They can also cover cold, bare floors to make a room feel more cozy.

Accessories add the finishing touch to any decorating project. But try to use objects that fit with the room's mood, color and theme.

With a little practice and careful attention to detail, you'll be able to create a beautiful space that is an expression of your own personal style.

Helpful Hint:

- If you want an object to stand out, such as a sculpture or vase, place it against a sharply contrasting color background. If you want to camouflage an object, like a piece of furniture that is too large for the space, place it in front of a similar colored background.

Money-Saving Idea:

- If you want to hang a group of framed prints together in a wall display, but the frames are mismatched styles and colors, use a can of spray paint to unify their appearance. Spray paint comes in a wide variety of colors and finishes. Simply remove the prints and glass, spray paint the frames and reassemble the pictures to create a beautiful, cohesive grouping.

A Shade Shy and a Valance Short

Window treatments dramatically affect the overall look of any room. There are hundreds of choices, including curtains, shades, blinds, shutters and valances. How do you decide which ones will work for your decorating project?

The most important thing to consider when choosing window treatments is the function they need to perform. Window coverings can provide privacy, block light, heat, cold or noise, as well as protect your furniture from the harsh rays of the sun. The main function for window treatments in a bedroom is usually privacy, but light and sound control can also be important. Make sure the window treatments you choose will perform the function you need.

Window coverings help soften the hard, rectangular lines of windows and help decorate your room. You can use them to create a focal point if your room doesn't have an attractive architectural feature. They can also camouflage problems with the size and shape of your windows, which we'll discuss in the Designer Tricks section of this book.

A room's mood is determined by the colors, the style of furniture and accessories, and the lighting that is used in the space. The window treatments you choose should also complement the color and style of your décor.

For example, if your décor is contemporary, you wouldn't choose country style café curtains for your room. You also wouldn't use formal velvet draperies in a casual country style room.

The fabric and hardware you choose will affect how formal or informal the window treatments will be. A swag made from tapestry fabric draped over an ornate metal pole is elegant and formal. But a swag made of cotton print fabric draped over a rustic wooden pole creates a more casual, informal look.

Another factor to keep in mind is that the window treatments should be suitable in scale with the size of the room. Floor to ceiling, heavy draperies would be out of scale in a tiny bedroom with small scale furniture.

Below is a list of some of the choices for window coverings that you might want to consider for your room.

Blinds: Some of the many choices of blinds that are available include bamboo roll-up blinds (shown at right) or match-stick pull-up blinds which are more casual, create a tropical or Asian mood and can be used in either a traditional or contemporary setting. But these blinds don't provide complete privacy.

Vertical blinds, shown in Figure 4 below, are typically used for informal, contemporary décor.

Figure 4   **Figure 5**

Venetian blinds (horizontal slats) are more informal and are made from wood for a traditional setting or metal for a contemporary look. Figure 5 shows an example of drapery panels over wooden Venetian blinds.

Shades: Roman shades, flat fabric shades that fold up in pleats, can be formal or informal, traditional or contemporary, depending on the fabric used. See Figure 6 on page 42.

Balloon shades (either pleated or gathered) are used in traditional décor, and can be formal or informal depending on the fabric chosen. An example of a pleated balloon shade is shown in Figure 7 on page 42.

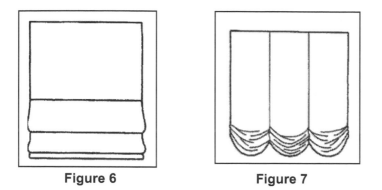

Figure 6   **Figure 7**

Shutters: Louvred wooden shutters, shown in Figure 8 below, are available in a variety of blade widths. Narrow blade shutters are more traditional and can be either formal or informal. Wide blade shutters work well for contemporary or tropical décor.

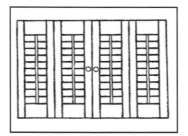

Figure 8

Draperies: Draperies (lined curtains) are made of heavier weight fabrics. They can be hung in a fixed position, called "dress draperies" or hung from hooks on traverse rods so they can be opened to provide light or closed for privacy. They can be used in combination with just about any of the other window treatments. Draperies can be formal or informal, traditional or contemporary, depending on the fabric used and how they are combined with other window treatments. See the example in Figure 5 on page 41.

Curtains: Curtains are unlined panels of fabric, either sheer or opaque, that can be pleated, gathered onto rods through rod pockets or hung from rings or tabs. They have a lighter, more casual feel than draperies. Café curtains are hung from rings and cover only the bottom part of the window for a casual look as shown in Figure 10 on page 44.

Valances: Valances can be made of fabric or wood (cornice) and can be formal or informal depending on their fabric and shape, as well as how they are combined with other treatments. See Figure 5 on page 41.

Remember to keep the elements of function, style and scale in mind when planning for your window treatments.

When choosing design motifs for curtain fabrics, upholstery fabrics, wall paper and floor coverings, it's best to use only one bold pattern in the room. This might be the fabric in your bedding or a design on an area rug. Good choices for secondary prints to use with your main pattern are smaller scale stripes, dots, checks and plaids that coordinate with your color scheme and style of décor.

Another way to create harmony in your room is by repeating a color or pattern several times throughout the space. You can do this by using the same fabric from your window treatments in accent pillows for your bed or chair, or in a tablecloth on a side table.

Window coverings don't have to be expensive. There are many creative options for no-sew curtains, using lengths of fabric or flat sheets to drape across the tops of your windows in the form of swags as shown in Figure 9 on page 44. You can also hang pillow cases or lace panels from clip-on rings, as shown in Figure 10 on page 44.

Figure 9   **Figure 10**

A few other creative solutions are listed below:

- Drape a round tablecloth over a rod or drape a square tablecloth diagonally over a rod for a window topper.

- Hang fabric napkins or lace handkerchiefs diagonally over a rod to form a valance, as shown in Figure 10.

- When using a length of fabric to create a swag curtain, as shown in Figure 9, hem the ends with iron-on, fusible hemming tape if you don't sew. Or cut the fabric long enough so that it puddles onto the floor and tuck the raw edges under so they don't show.

- Add colorful trim (braid, beaded, fringe, tassel, etc.) to plain curtain panels, or stamp or stencil designs on them using acrylic paints.

- Hang a flat lace panel from a rod using clip-on rings.

- Attach shelves inside a window to hold rows of colored glass bottles in a variety of shapes and sizes.

- Hang a silk or dried floral swag along the top of the window instead of a valance.

Be sure to check out new ideas in books at your local fabric or craft store. There are also a wide variety of inexpensive, ready-made curtain panels, valances and window shades available at discount stores and home improvement stores.

Just remember to consider the function you need the window coverings to perform, as well as the style and scale of your room.

Don't forget to re-design your window treatments when you re-design your room. They can make a dramatic change in the finished look.

Fun Ideas:

- Windowpane mirrors (a piece of wall art that looks like a window with a mirror behind it) can create the illusion of a real window on a windowless wall, reflecting light into your space. They also help to add architectural interest to the room and come in a variety of shapes and sizes, including rectangular, round and arched.

- It's easy to make a roll-up shade using heavy-duty cardboard tubes approximately 1-1/4" in diameter (like the ones inside a roll of gift wrapping paper).

First, measure the inside width of your window and cut two cardboard tubes 1/2" shorter than this measurement. Next, measure the height of the window and add 8" to this measurement. Cut your fabric this length and 1" wider than the tubes.

Press under 1/2" along each side edge of the fabric and hem with 1/2" fusible (iron-on) tape. Hot-glue the top edge of the fabric to one of the tubes. Roll the fabric until the tube is completely covered, then hot-glue in place. Repeat with the other tube on the bottom edge of the fabric.

Roll up the shade to desired length and tie a few inches from each end with 1/2" ribbon looped over the top and bottom of the shade.

Insert a tension rod through the top tube and install inside your window.

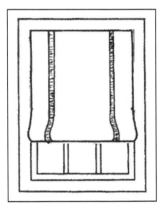

Shedding a Little Light

Ineffective lighting is another common decorating problem that can affect the function of a room and make it feel uninviting. Proper lighting is not only functional, it can add a magical touch that can bring your room to life. It is the final element you will use to make your space more comfortable and beautiful.

Plan the lighting for your room the same way you planned all the other aspects of your design, by considering the function the lighting needs to perform and the mood you want it to create. Also check to see that your lighting is balanced throughout the space.

Function:

When planning for lighting, be sure to provide adequate light for the tasks you'll be performing in your room, such as reading, deskwork or hobbies that require good visibility, such as sewing or crafting. Table lamps, floor lamps and wall-mounted swing-arm lamps are good choices for task lighting.

There should also be enough general (or ambient) lighting in the room to prevent it from being too dark. Use fixtures such as chandeliers, torchieres (floor lamps that shine light upward), sconces and track lights for general lighting. It's a good idea to have a dimmer switch installed on these fixtures so you can vary the level of light in the room.

Mood:

There are three ways you can use lighting to influence the mood of a room: by the general feeling of the illumination (how bright or dim the lighting is), by the style of the light fixtures and by the use of accent lights.

The general illumination has the greatest effect on the room's mood. A brightly lit room projects a more work oriented mood, such as the light needed in a kitchen. A dimly lit room is more intimate and romantic, such as the level of light desirable in a bedroom. Decide what mood you want to create in your space in order to choose the type of lighting that will work best for your needs.

The light fixtures that you select express a certain style or mood. Some fixtures, such as table lamps, chandeliers and sconces, are more traditional and some are more contemporary in style. Some are lavish and ornate; others are simple and stark. As with the furniture you selected, lighting fixtures should complement the mood and style of your décor. For example, modern table lamps would not be suitable in mood or style for a Victorian style bedroom.

You can provide accents of light in specific areas of a room to add a dramatic touch. This type of lighting is called accent lighting. A few examples are listed below:

- Use a floor can to shine light up through the foliage of a large plant

- Showcase a piece of art using a picture light

- Use low-voltage rope lights (tiny lights inside a flexible plastic tube) on top of bookcases to provide indirect lighting

- Use a lamp on a table to brighten a dark corner

- Use rope lights inside shelving units or curio cabinets to highlight collectibles

- Use rope lights behind each curtain valance to provide a pleasant glow at night and highlight the fabric of the draperies in your room

Accent lighting not only highlights special artwork and brightens dark corners, it adds drama and interest to your overall design.

Place a floor can light behind a large plant to shine light up through the foliage.

Lighting Fixture Choices:

The different lighting elements in a room need to work together to provide the right amount of light needed to perform specific tasks, as well as to achieve the overall mood you want in the room. Consider the following when planning for the lighting in your space:

- Add variety to your lighting plan. Use different types of lighting fixtures for different tasks. Some of the many options available include: table lamps, sconces, chandeliers, floor lamps, recessed down lights, indirect lighting, low voltage rope lights and floor cans. Check out the many options available at your local home improvement store.

- Have the illumination in your room flow in different directions. Some fixtures project light upward (a torchiere or floor can light), some downward (ceiling mounted or recessed can lights in the ceiling) and some project light in all directions (a chandelier or table lamp with a translucent shade).

- Position lighting fixtures at different heights, from ceiling to floor—some at the ceiling, some on tables and some on the floor. Try to distribute them evenly around the room to create a more balanced feel.

- Plan for different levels of illumination in different parts of the room. Some areas should be bright (for reading), some less bright (for watching television). Use dimmer switches on general lighting, as well as task lighting to control the amount of light you want at different times.

Lighting is an important element when decorating your space. Be sure to give it the time and attention it deserves. Proper lighting can dramatically affect the function, mood and beauty of any space. Make your room sparkle with the magic of lighting.

Creative Ideas for Customizing
Table Lamps and Shades

Not only are table lamps functional for providing task lighting, they can help decorate your space. A lamp on a bedside table can provide a cozy welcome. A small lamp can also light up a dark corner and showcase collectibles arranged on a table. Even if a lamp is not lit, it adds to the overall décor, especially if it is customized to match your design.

Giving new life to old lamps and lampshades is easy. It's also a good way to save a few decorating dollars. Use the following ideas to refurbish or customize old lamps and shades that you already have or ones that you find at garage sales or even new ones that are on sale but don't quite match your current style.

For older lamps, make sure the wiring is in good condition. If not, have them rewired before using them.

Refinishing a Lamp Base:

Just about any lamp base can be painted. There are hundreds of spray paint products on the market today for covering any material from porcelain to plastic to metal. They include a wide selection of paint finishes, such as stone, pewter, bronze and terracotta. You will need an adult to purchase spray paint for you and supervise the painting. It's best to wear a mask while using spray paint.

To paint your lamp base, cover the light bulb socket (and any other parts of the base that you don't want painted) with masking tape and newspaper. Following the directions on the can, spray paint the lamp base and let dry.

After painting the base, you can add even more details by using stencils, decals or decoupage. You can also drape your lamp base with an elegant tassel or glue on beads, buttons or faux jewels.

If you don't want to paint the base, cover it with fabric. Simply measure the lamp base from the neck, down one side, across the bottom and back up the opposite side to the neck. Add about 4 or 5 inches to this measurement to allow for tucking under the raw edges at the top. Cut a square piece of fabric this size.

Lay the piece of fabric on a flat surface, wrong-side up. Place the lamp base in the center of the fabric, cut a tiny hole for the electrical cord to go through, and gather up the fabric around the neck of the lamp, tucking under the raw edges of the fabric. Secure the fabric by tying a piece of ribbon or jute around the neck of the lamp.

You can also change the fabric on the lamp to match your décor for different seasons or holidays.

Customizing a Lamp Shade:

Lampshades come in hundreds of different shapes and sizes. You can buy inexpensive, plain shades at home improvement stores or discount stores and customize them for your décor. You can also refurbish shades you already own or have purchased second-hand.

The following is a list of ideas for customizing your shades:

- Smooth lampshades can be painted with a sponge brush and acrylic paints or spray paint. You'll need an adult to purchase spray paint and supervise the painting. Wear a mask when using spray paint.

- Glue fabric appliqué designs that are found at craft or fabric stores onto smooth shades.

- Use stencils or rubber stamps and acrylic paint to decorate a smooth shade.

- Glue on colorful buttons, crocheted doilies or tiny satin ribbon roses for a feminine touch.

- Cover the entire shade by gluing on silk flowers.

- Glue ribbon, rickrack, braided trims, tassel trim, fur trim, feather trim or beaded trim to the top and/or bottom edges.

- Decoupage paper print cutouts or copies of photos onto the shade using a decoupage medium found at craft stores.

- Using a corsage pin, punch holes through a dark, opaque shade in a simple design such as a heart or star, so the light will shine through the holes. Simply draw your shape on a piece of paper and tape it in position on the shade. Punch holes through the shade, about 1/4" apart, along the lines of the drawn pattern shape. Repeat the pattern several times on the shade.

- Add a gathered skirt of fabric or lace over a shade.

These are just a few ideas for adding a customized look to your décor. Have fun experimenting with these techniques, so you can add your own personal touch to your room.

Conflict or Harmony

Whatever style of furnishings and color scheme you choose, your goal is to create harmony in your space. This means that all the décor in the room (the furniture, accessories, window treatments and floor and wall coverings) should harmonize with the mood you have chosen for the room. Striving for harmony in your design will help create that "pulled together" look you see in professionally decorated spaces.

Selecting Furniture Styles:

The style of furniture you select will determine the mood of your space. Do you want the room to be casual or formal, modern or traditional, romantic or tailored? If you're planning to use furniture you already own, then you'll need to plan your mood around those pieces.

If you want a contemporary mood for your room, and all your furniture is a rustic country style, then you'll either need to select a different mood to fit your existing furniture, alter the look of your furniture with paint or upholstery, or purchase furniture that is more suitable for the mood you want to create in order to achieve a more harmonious feel for your space.

If the wooden furniture pieces you want to use are similar but different styles and the wood tones don't match, try to unify them by painting them and changing the hardware (draw pulls and knobs) to match.

Tips for Painting Wooden Furniture:

- Wash the surface to remove any dirt or grease using a damp (not soaking) cloth and a mild solution of water and detergent. Let dry.
- Sand the surface lightly with fine grit sandpaper and remove any dust with a damp paper towel.
- Apply a coat of primer, using a paint brush or sponge roller. Check with your local paint store for the appropriate primer to cover the current finish, whether it is oil-based paint, water-based paint, stain, shellac, etc. Let primer coat dry.
- Lightly sand the surface again and remove any dust.
- Ask the expert at your local paint store which type of paint is best for your project (oil-based or water-based). Apply your paint with a paint brush or sponge roller or use cans of spray paint and let dry. Add a second coat of paint if needed.

If you want to use mismatched upholstered furniture pieces that are fairly similar in style, cover them with matching or coordinating furniture slipcovers. There are many affordable choices for slipcovers available at discount stores and home improvement stores, as well as on-line.

These covers also come in handy if you like to change the style of your room seasonally, from a heavier, winter feel to a lighter, summer look.

Scale:

Another important aspect to consider when selecting the furniture for your room is scale. Scale refers to the size of a piece of furniture in relation to the size of the other furniture in the room, or in relation to the size of the room itself. For example, a queen-size bed in a very small bedroom is out of scale with the room. A large table lamp is not in scale when placed on a tiny bedside table.

The easiest way to keep all the furniture in your room in scale is to start by choosing the most important piece first, such as the sofa for a living room or the dining table in a dining room. If you make sure that this piece is in scale with the room, and check carefully that all the other pieces of furniture are in scale with this piece, then you will have harmony in scale for the entire room. Since you'll be decorating your bedroom, the bed will be the most important piece to keep in scale with the size of your room.

After choosing the mood or theme you want for your room, select pieces of furniture that fit with the style of your décor and are in scale with the size of your room in order to achieve a harmonious design.

Choosing Accessories:

The accessories you choose for your decorating project will also affect the mood of the room. As with the furniture selection, be sure your accessories fit with the style or theme of your décor. For example, you wouldn't want to hang a stuffed deer head on the wall in your romantic, feminine bedroom, or display a delicate porcelain figurine on a rustic, barn-wood shelf.

Also remember that some decorating styles call for more accessories, such as country or cottage, and others require fewer, such as contemporary. Include the number of accessories that you feel are appropriate for the decorating style you have chosen.

Another way to create harmony and continuity in your decorating scheme is to repeat a color or pattern at least three times in the room. Whether it is a type of metal finish, a fabric print or a geometric shape, try to repeat it several times throughout the space. If the drawer pulls on your dresser are bronze, repeat that finish in the lamp bases and picture frames. Use the same fabric from your window treatments in accent pillows on your bed or a tablecloth on a side table.

Try to choose accessories that work with the mood of the room and are in harmony with the color and style of the décor. Pay close attention to the mood each object projects. Does it match the style of your room? With practice, you can train your eye to look for these details.

Choosing a Harmonious Color Scheme:

The colors you use on the walls, as well as for accents, should also be appropriate for the decorating style or theme in your room. For example, sunny yellow, bright red and cobalt blue would be good choices for a French Country style, but not for an English Cottage style, which calls for soft pinks and greens. (See page 27 and 28 for a few specific decorating style color schemes.)

If you're not sure what colors are suitable for the decorating style you've chosen, do some research at the library or on-line. The results will be well worth your effort.

The use of color is a very powerful decorating tool, which can affect the way you feel when you are in the room. If you want a soothing mood for your bedroom or bath, don't paint the walls an energizing color like orange. The warm colors: reds, yellows and oranges are more energizing. The cool colors: blues, greens and violets are more calming, especially the pastel versions. Neutral colors, such as beige and taupe are also more soothing. Paint the walls in your room a color that will evoke the mood you want.

When deciding on a color scheme, choose colors that are harmonious with the style of the décor you've chosen, as well as the mood you want to create.

Using Appropriate Lighting:

The lighting used in your space should also be appropriate for the mood you have chosen. Not only should the style of the light fixtures be harmonious with the rest of the décor, but the amount of light they produce should create the desired mood.

The lighting for a bedroom should be softer and more subtle than the bright lights required in a work space, such as a kitchen or craft room. However, since your bedroom is also your workspace for homework or other projects, you will need a variety of light levels in different parts of your room, depending on the tasks you need to perform.

And don't forget to add accent lighting to brighten any dark corners in your space or highlight special artwork. These creative touches add an extra sparkle that can bring your room to life.

The Joy of Harmony:

In order to achieve harmony in your space, all the elements you choose for your room: the furniture, color scheme, window treatments, accessories and lighting, should work together to create the overall mood and style you envisioned.

If you pay close attention to the details of your design and practice your observation skills, you will sense when a particular object and its scale, style and color are not harmonious with the rest of your décor.

Your decorating goal should be to create a space that functions well and adds beauty and joy to your life.

Don't worry about decorating trends and fads. Use the colors, furniture styles and accessories that you love, and you will have a space that is both comfortable and beautiful.

Designer Tricks

There are many design "tricks of the trade" that you can use to create optical illusions to make your room appear different than it actually is. Whether you want to change the size or shape of your room or windows, or want to double an image, or make an object disappear, follow the guidelines below to help camouflage the negative features and highlight the positive features in your room.

Changing Room Dimensions

If you aren't happy with the dimensions or architectural features of your room, there are several designer tricks you can use to change its appearance through optical illusions.

Does the room feel too small or too narrow? Does the ceiling feel too low? Knowing how to choose the right wall treatments, furniture, window coverings and flooring can make all the difference. Choose the options below that best fit your room's needs:

To make a small room feel larger:

- Use small-scale furniture.

- Use solid color upholstery fabrics or fabrics with small design motifs.

- Avoid crowding the room with too much furniture.

- Paint the walls a light color to make them appear to recede. Paint doors and trim the same color as the walls to unify the space.

- The window treatment color should blend with the wall color, not contrast with it. Use either a solid color or small print for the fabric. If the curtains are made of print fabric, match the background color to the walls.

- Use small scale window treatments.

- Don't break up the floor space with area rugs.

To make a large room feel smaller:

- Select large-scale furniture and use plenty of pieces to keep the room from feeling empty.

- Light colored upholstery will make furniture appear bigger and fill the space better. Bright colors and bold design motifs also make furniture seem larger.

- Paint the walls a darker color and try to break up the space by painting wall moldings, baseboards and trim around doors and windows in a contrasting color.

- Use a different wall treatment on one or more of the walls, such as a painted accent wall, a wall mural or wallpaper.

- Use big and/or elaborate window treatments. Dark window treatments, like dark wall paint, will make the room appear smaller, but light window treatments will contrast with the darker walls to break up the space. Either choice is fine.

- Break up the floor space with area rugs. Large, bold design motifs for area rugs are fine as long as they don't compete with a different bold design pattern on the walls or furniture.

To make a narrow room feel wider:

- Paint the end walls a darker color to make them appear to "advance" and use light colors on the long walls to make them appear to "recede".

- Use a striped rug with the stripes running across the width of the room.

- Hang several framed prints in a horizontal row across one or both of the narrow (end) walls.

- Cover one of the long walls with floor-to-ceiling mirrors, which will appear to double the width of the room.

To make a low ceiling appear higher:

- Accentuate the vertical lines in the room by removing any horizontal moldings or paint them the same color as the walls.

- If using wallpaper, apply vertical patterns from floor to ceiling.

- Window treatments should also continue from floor to ceiling to avoid cutting the vertical height.

- Paint the ceiling a light color (white is best) to make it appear to recede.

- Darker colors on the floors make them appear to be lower than they actually are.

To make a high ceiling seem lower:

- Accentuate the horizontal lines on the walls by painting the horizontal trim (crown molding, chair rail and baseboards) in a contrasting color.

- Use contrasting wallpaper prints and/or paint colors above and below the chair rail, dividing the walls into two horizontal planes. If you don't have a chair rail, use a wallpaper border to divide the two treatments.

- Paint the crown molding the same color as the ceiling, or use a wallpaper border, matching the background color of the border to the ceiling color.

- Paint the ceiling a darker color than the walls.

- Lighter colors on the floors make them appear to be higher than they actually are.

Changing Window Dimensions with Curtains

Make a short window appear taller by adding a valance above it, starting the bottom edge of the valance just below the top edge of the window, and the top of the valance extends onto the wall space above the window.

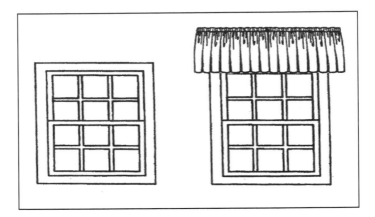

Make a tall window appear shorter by adding a valance, which starts near the top edge of the window and drops down to cover the top part of the window.

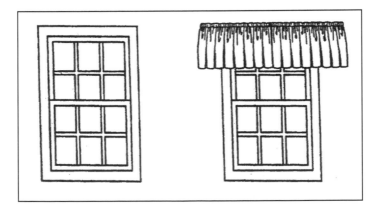

Make a wide window appear narrower by adding curtain panels to each side, starting close to the outside edge of the window and extending inside to cover some of its width.

Make a narrow window appear wider by adding curtain panels to each side of the window, which start at the side edges of the window and extend beyond the outer edges of the window onto the wall.

Adjust the heights of different size windows on the same wall by adding a valance that extends across the tops of both windows to make them appear the same height. Adjust their widths by adding curtain panels to each side to make them appear the same.

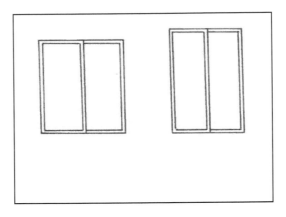

Designer Tricks
Using Mirrors

The unique characteristics of mirrors make them a very creative and useful decorating tool. Their reflective surfaces can increase the amount of light in the space, create optical illusions to make your room appear larger, or double the impact of any object they reflect.

Everyone knows that using wall-to-wall mirrors can make a room appear larger. Replacing the wooden sliding doors on your closet with ones covered with mirrors can produce a similar effect.

Decoratively framed mirrors can add a touch of elegance and style to any room, as well as being functional. A large framed mirror hung above a chest can be the centerpiece of a focal point. You can also hang a group of small, framed mirrors together on a wall to create architectural interest.

Windowpane mirrors (a piece of wall art that looks like a window with a mirror behind it) can create the illusion of a real window on a blank wall. They come in a wide variety of shapes, sizes and decorating styles, and work great with any décor.

If your desk faces a wall without a window, hang a mirror on the wall in front of you that will reflect a more pleasing view behind you, such as a piece of artwork or a window with a view.

You can double the impact of your artwork or windows by placing mirrors opposite them to repeat the image from another angle in the room. Whenever you hang a mirror in a room, always check to make sure that it is reflecting a pleasant image.

In addition to being attractive accessories, framed mirrors are also functional. Hanging a mirror in your room makes it easy to check your appearance before leaving. Just be sure to hang it at an appropriate height for viewing.

Mirrors can also be used to make objects "disappear". If you have an unsightly post standing in the middle of your room, which cannot be removed because it is structurally necessary, consider having it covered with mirrors. They will reflect the objects in the room, making the post less noticeable. The same trick works for an over-scaled, rectangular chest or table.

The Power of Illusions

When used effectively, these designer tricks can dramatically change the appearance of a room's scale or proportions to camouflage negative architectural features or accentuate positive features.

Which negative features in your room do you want to change? Which ones do you want to highlight? Now that you know how to use these designer tricks, you'll be able to make your room look its best.

What's Your Style?

Do you already have a clear idea about what style of décor you prefer? If not, then you need to do a bit of research. A good way to accomplish this is to visit furniture stores, wall paper stores, fabric stores and paint stores.

While there, make notes about the prints, colors, finishes and styles that attract your attention. What is it about them that you like? Also make a few notes about the ones you don't like and why they don't appeal to you. You'll soon see a pattern developing for a particular style and palette of colors that you prefer.

Whenever you see a picture in a decorating magazine or catalogue that represents a style or color you like, tear it out and place it in an idea file. You can have categories for accessories, furniture, color schemes, window treatments and any other decorating subjects that you want to add.

This file will help define your style preference, as well as provide decorating ideas for future projects.

Common Decorating Styles

The following is a brief description of some of the most common decorating styles used today. Which one appeals to you?

Country:

This style, ranging from English cottage to American farmhouse, has a more rustic theme that's all about casual comfort. It includes lots of texture, such as weathered woods and rough stone mixed with simple cotton fabrics in old-fashioned floral prints, plaids and denim. Window treatments are casual and simple. Accessories include antique collectibles, quilts, old toys and tools, and dried flowers or informal bouquets.

Traditional:

This formal decorating style features heirloom-quality cabinetry, ornate moldings and fine fabrics, such as velvets, damasks and silks. Furniture is hand-carved from rich, dark wood, like cherry or mahogany.

The color scheme is drawn from deep, rich colors featuring navy, burgundy and forest green. Ornate accessories include shiny finishes, such as cut crystal, polished brass or silver as well as oil paintings in frames that are heavily carved and gilded.

Contemporary:

This style features furniture with clean lines, simple contours and strong horizontal elements. It calls for very few accessories, which are selected for their bold color and sculptural appeal.

Color schemes include neutrals, black and white, accented with bright, bold colors. Shots of color are introduced in the form of an accent wall or in a geometric pattern on an area rug or throw pillows.

Floor and table lamps have straight lines and metallic finishes or bold colors and sculptural bases.

Transitional:

This style incorporates furnishings from both traditional and contemporary décor. Transitional rooms are more casual than the formal traditional style with the less cluttered feel of the contemporary style.

Choose large, comfortable pieces of furniture that have the simple, straight lines found in contemporary décor. Add more traditional pieces that have soft, curved lines, like carved wooden tables and chairs. As in contemporary décor, limit the number of accessories, using just a few outstanding pieces.

Use objects that contrast in style, such as antique plates and contemporary paintings.

Eclectic:

Eclectic decorating mixes several different styles. The key is to use other elements, such as color and texture, to coordinate pieces from different periods.

It includes a harmonious mix of furniture, fixtures, and accessories that appeal to you. The most successful eclectic rooms incorporate only two or three different styles, but use a common decorating theme, such as color or shape to tie them all together.

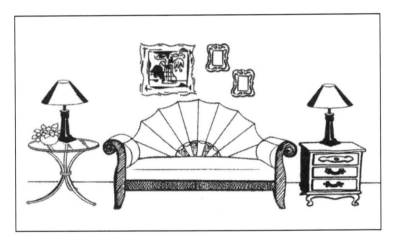

What's your decorating style? With a little research you'll be able to discover the furniture styles, finishes, patterns and colors that appeal to you. Then your room will be a reflection of who you are and what you like.

Fun Ideas for Theme Rooms

Your room should reflect your interests and personality. Choosing a theme can make it easier to decide on the colors, style of furnishings and accessories you want to use.

Simply choose a theme, whether it's an activity you like to do, such as dancing or sports; a place you've been or would like to go, like a country, state or city; or a time era you really admire.

Next, gather everything you can think of to support your theme, including paint colors, fabric prints, bedding, furniture, window treatments, artwork and accessories. This might require a bit of research at the library or online to help make your theme more authentic.

The decorating styles and color schemes listed on pages 27 and 28 are examples of theme room designs. A few more fun possibilities are listed below:

Location Theme: Paris, France

Joie de Vivre

Paint the walls a pale pink color, and your wooden furniture pieces black for contrast. Paint a mural of the Eiffel tower on one wall. Stencil the words "joie de vivre" on the wall over your bed.

Add a tiny bistro table and chair in the corner if you have the space. Hang frilly white curtains or pink and white striped curtain panels over the windows.

Your bedding can be made from pink and white striped fabric with lots of throw pillows in white, black and various shades of pink—either solid fabrics or small-scale plaids, dots, checks or prints. Add a white eyelet dust ruffle.

Don't forget the artwork: a black and white Picasso print or line drawings of Paris street scenes in a black frames would really pop against those pink walls.

Time Era: The Flower-Power '60's

This style is all about neon colors (orange, pink, green, yellow and turquoise), flowers, peace, love and beads. If you really like color, you might choose a sunny yellow for your walls.

Use the other bright colors for accents, such as painted furniture, vases, picture frames and lamp bases. Paint or stencil colorful flowers, hearts and the word "Love" on one or two of the walls, but don't overdo it. You don't want your room to feel like a graffiti nightmare.

Your bedding can be a bright solid color like turquoise, with contrasting bright orange, yellow or green throw pillows in fabric or fake fur.

Hang a colorful beaded curtain behind the headboard of your bed or hang it from the ceiling as a room divider to section off a sitting area filled with bright colored floor pillows in floral fabrics or fake fur.

Use tie-dyed fabric for curtains and throw pillows for the bed or floor.

A Vacation You Enjoyed: Hawaii

Paint the walls a medium blue color to simulate the ocean. Your bedding can be a tropical island or beach-theme print fabric. Pick up one of the brighter colors from your bedding, like red or hot pink, to use as an accent color for throw pillows and other accessories. Display some of the souvenirs you collected on your vacation, such as sea shells or leis. Frame a collection of attractive postcards or favorite photos from your trip.

Use rattan furniture pieces if you can find a few. Hang a couple of large framed prints of Hawaiian beach scenes on the walls. Or paint a tropical island beach scene on one wall, complete with palm trees, sand and ocean.

Use gauzy white curtains over matchstick blinds, for a tropical feel. Add a real or fake palm tree in the corner, if you have space for it, to complete your beach design.

An Activity You Enjoy: Dance

If you are passionate about ballet, you can design a truly romantic room for your retreat. Paint the walls a pale lavender color. Paint your furniture white and sand the edges for a worn, shabby chic look.

Your bedding can be a shiny, satin-like fabric, also in pale lavender or lavender print. Use lots of satin throw pillows in white, lavender and deep purple on the bed.

Drape yards of white tulle over a curved curtain rod hung over your bed and let it hang down on each side of the bed as shown in the drawing below.

Hang several large, framed prints of ballerinas on your walls. Or paint a mural of a ballerina or ballet shoes on one wall.

Drape yards of white tulle over the window frames and let it puddle onto the floor, as shown in the drawing on page 9. Use white cellular shades or blinds for privacy.

Add accessories in shiny brass or crystal for accents throughout your room. A small crystal and brass chandelier would be the perfect finishing touch of elegance.

These are just a few ideas to spark your creativity. Plan a theme for your room based on a favorite activity, hobby, unique location or era. It will help make the time you spend there more enjoyable.

Quick Change Decorating

Are you tired of the same old décor, but don't have the time or budget for a major redo? Try a few of the following tips to give your room a quick change without spending a lot of money or time.

- Instead of painting the entire room, paint just an accent wall. Use a totally different color that coordinates with your existing furniture or bedding, but perhaps a bit more bold.

- Re-arrange the furniture in your room using the decorating guidelines presented in this book. You'll get a whole new look for zero dollars and very little time.

- If your bedding is looking faded and tired, replace it with a new set. You can find inexpensive bedding sets at many discount stores. A new bed spread can change the look of your room with a new design theme and colors. Just make sure it coordinates with the current wall color in your room if you're not planning to paint.

- If your upholstered furniture pieces are looking a bit worn or dated, cover them with slip covers. This is also an easy and inexpensive way to change the look of your room with the seasons, from a heavier winter look to a lighter summer feel.

- Use some of the creative ideas listed on pages 43 - 46 to create new window treatments. You can also change their look seasonally by removing heavier winter draperies and using a simple valance over sheer curtains or blinds.

- Change the throw pillows in your room. Whether you buy them, make your own, or add trims to store-bought pillows, they can help change the color and style of your room. You can change them out with each season or add holiday pillows for extra punch. Throw pillows can create a whole new look for very little cost.

- Draping a throw across the bed or over a chair can add new color, texture and style to your room. It can also hide an unsightly stain or tear in the upholstery. During the winter, it provides a cozy touch that is also functional in case you feel a chill.

- Adding an area rug is another easy and inexpensive way to change the look of a room. Rugs are sold at a variety of discount and home improvement stores in a wide range of prices. They can add color and texture, help define a conversation area, make a room feel cozier, or completely change the room's style.

  Use darker, more vibrant colors in thick, plush carpets for a winter feel and lighter, airy colors in light-weight woven rugs for a summer look.

- Accessories are the finishing touches in any room. Rearranging these pieces can create a quick decorating change. Collect similar items that you have scattered throughout your room and display them together in a group to create a dramatic focal point or emphasize a theme.

- A new piece of wall art might be just the focal point your room needs. You can find inexpensive framed prints at many discount stores, furniture resale stores or garage sales. It might inspire you to take your room's décor in a whole new direction. Changing the wall décor is an easy way to give your room a quick makeover.

- Add inexpensive new accessories, such as colorful baskets or pretty, fabric-covered boxes to provide decorative storage, or plants and greenery (real or silk) to add softness and life to the space.

- Change out the lampshades in your room. You can purchase inexpensive shades at many home improvement or discount stores.

  Or spruce up a lampshade you found at a garage sale or one you already own by painting it, covering it with fabric or simply adding trims such as beading or braid.

  You can do the same thing with most lamp bases for a whole new look. See the instructions for customizing lamp bases and shades on pages 52 - 54.

- Add accent lighting to create drama and brighten any dark corners. An inexpensive floor can placed behind a tall plant will create highlights and patterns on the walls and ceiling. Add a small picture light to emphasize a special piece of wall art. Place a string of low-voltage rope lights inside a curio cabinet to showcase collectibles. Refer to page 49 for more accent lighting suggestions. These are all quick, low-budget tricks that can add a bit of sparkle to any room.

Make your room an expression of your own personal style. Changing your décor doesn't have to cost a bundle. All it takes is a little time and effort and a lot of creativity.

Creative Ideas for Storage

An organized, clutter-free room promotes a feeling of order and peace—a valuable commodity in today's chaotic world. Clutter has a way of sneaking up on us gradually until we feel overwhelmed and helpless in its wake.

It's important to get rid of the clutter in your room and keep only the items you need and love. That's why every decorating make-over starts off by clearing everything out of the space, so you can start with a clean slate. You are much less likely to bring the clutter back in to your freshly decorated room.

After getting rid of everything but your "absolute must haves", you'll need to find creative ways to store or display them. This sounds like a daunting task, but it can actually be fun if you take a creative approach.

Buying containers or storage units to store all the items you need to keep can be expensive. One way to make the most efficient use of your storage budget is to buy containers or furniture units that will satisfy your storage needs and decorate your room as well.

The following is a list of some creative storage ideas for your room.

- Baskets are inexpensive but effective storage containers that can also add to your décor. They can hold magazines beside your favorite reading chair or craft supplies in a shelving unit. Place them on top of armoires or entertainment centers or underneath end tables to hold items that aren't used frequently. Hang baskets on the wall to hold magazines, homework papers or keys.

- Use old trunks instead of bedside tables. They can hold extra blankets or toys and games.

- Use small chests of drawers instead of beside tables to provide more storage.

- Old suitcases stacked on top of each other can work as a chairside table as well as storage (bolt them together to make them more stable).

- If you're planning to buy an ottoman, get a storage ottoman.

- Skirted tables (rectangular, square or round with a floor-length table cloth) can hide storage containers underneath.

- Bookcases or shelving units can hold decorative boxes for storing small items.

- If you need to buy bookcases, get the tallest ones your ceiling height will accommodate to get the maximum amount of storage for the least amount of floor space.

- Consider adding a shelf around the entire perimeter of the room at door height to store books, your treasured collectibles and attractive storage containers.

- Instead of a bench at the foot of the bed, choose a sturdy chest of drawers that can double as a bench, as well as storage.

- Lean a wooden ladder against the wall to hold quilts or throws. You can create an attractive display and free up lots of space in the closet.

- Use vintage doorknobs on the wall to hang a few pretty necklaces or evening purses. This display can do double duty as wall art.

- Cover storage boxes or round hat boxes with wallpaper or fabric and place them on top of an armoire or stack them on the floor.

- If your floor space is limited, consider getting a platform bed with drawers underneath instead of using a bed and dresser. Another choice is a combination loft bed with chest of drawers and desk underneath.

Get creative with your storage units and containers. They will help keep you organized and decorate your room at the same time.

Putting It All Together

Your room should be your sanctuary—a haven from the frantic pace of the world outside. We all want our living spaces to be functional, comfortable and beautiful.

Taking the time to create a plan for how your room needs to function and providing the necessary furniture and lighting to meet your needs will make it more enjoyable and relaxing.

Adding beauty to your living space with colors you love and furniture and accessories that you find appealing will have a positive affect on your mood and add joy to your life.

Use the suggestions, tips and fun ideas presented in this book to create a more attractive and inviting space.

Forget about decorating trends and fads. Make your room a reflection of who you are.

Happy decorating!!!

Index

About the Author

Gloria Hander Lyons has channeled 30 years of training and hands-on experience in the areas of art, interior decorating, crafting and event planning into writing creative how-to books. Her books cover a wide range of topics including decorating your home, cooking, planning weddings and tea parties, crafting and self-publishing. She has designed original craft projects featured in magazines, such as *Better Homes and Gardens, McCall's, Country Handcrafts* and *Crafts*.

She teaches interior decorating, self-publishing and wedding planning classes at her local community college. Much to her family's delight, her kitchen is in non-stop test mode, creating recipes for new cookbooks.

Visit her website for free craft ideas, decorating and event planning tips and tasty recipes at: www.BlueSagePress.com.

Ordering Information

To order additional copies of this book, send check or money order payable to:

 Blue Sage Press
48 Borondo Pines
La Marque, TX 77568

Cost for this edition is $7.95 per book plus $3.50 shipping and handling for the first book and $1.50 for each additional book shipped to the same address (U.S. currency only).

Texas residents add 8.25% sales tax to total order amount.

To pay by credit card or get a complete list of books written by Gloria Hander Lyons, visit our website at:

www.BlueSagePress.com

Other Books by Gloria Hander Lyons

- *Easy Microwave Desserts in a Mug*
- *Easy Microwave Desserts in a Mug for Kids*
- *No Rules-Just Fun Decorating*
- *Ten Common Home Decorating Mistakes & How To Avoid Them*
- *Decorating Basics: For Men Only!*
- *If Teapots Could Talk—Fun Ideas for Tea Parties*
- *The Super-Bride's Guide for Dodging Wedding Pitfalls*
- *Designs That Sell: How To Make Your Home Show Better and Sell Faster*
- *A Taste of Lavender: Delectable Treats with an Exotic Floral Flavor*
- *Lavender Sensations: Fragrant Herbs for Home & Bath*
- *Self-Publishing on a Budget: A Do-It-All-Yourself Guide*
- *Hand Over the Chocolate & No One Gets Hurt! The Chocolate-Lover's Cookbook*
- *The Secret Ingredient: Tasty Recipes with an Unusual Twist*
- *Flamingos, Poodle Skirts & Red Hots: Creative Theme Party Ideas*
- *Quick Gifts From the Kitchen: No Cooking Required*
- *40 Favorite Impossible Pies: Main Dishes & Desserts*
- *A Taste of Memories: Comforting Foods From Our Past*
- *Pearls of Wisdom For Creating a Joyful Life*
- *What's Up With That? Humorous Short Stories About Life in Modern-Day America*

For a complete list of all our fun how-to books, visit:
www.BlueSagePress.com

Or write to request a free book catalog:

Blue Sage Press
48 Borondo Pines
La Marque, TX 77568

Made in the USA
Lexington, KY
05 January 2014